D1644521

CITY CYCLING
COPENHAGEN

Rapha.

Thames & Hudson

Created by Andrew Edwards and Max Leonard of
Tandem London, a design, print and editorial studio

Thanks to Simon Væth for illustrations; Mary Embry
and Mikael Colville-Andersen of Copenhagenize
Design Co; and Claus Schmidt Andersen of Larry vs
Harry, makers of the finest cargo bikes

First published in the United Kingdom in 2013 by
Thames & Hudson Ltd, 181A High Holborn, London WC1V 7QX

City Cycling Copenhagen © 2013 Andrew Edwards and Max Leonard
Illustrations © 2013 Thames & Hudson Ltd, London and Rapha Racing Ltd

Designed by Andrew Edwards

Illustrations by Simon Væth, simonvaeth.dk

British Library Cataloguing-in-Publication Data
A catalogue record for this book is available from the British Library

ISBN 978-0-500-29102-3

Printed and bound in China by Everbest Printing Co Ltd

To find out about all our publications, please visit
www.thamesandhudson.com. There you can subscribe
to our e-newsletter, browse or download our current catalogue,
and buy any titles that are in print.

CONTENTS

HOW TO USE THIS GUIDE

This Copenhagen volume of the City Cycling series is designed to give you the confidence to explore the city by bike at your own pace. On the front flaps is a locator map of the whole city to help you orient yourself. We've divided the city up into four different neighbourhoods: City (p. 10); Nørrebro (p. 18); Vesterbro (p. 24); and Christianshavn and Islands Brygge (p. 30). All are easily accessible by bike, and are full of cafés, bars, galleries, museums, shops and parks. Each area is mapped in detail, and our recommendations for places of interest and where to fuel up on coffee and cake, as well as where to find a Wi-Fi connection, are marked. Take a pootle round on your bike and see what suits you.

The neighbourhood maps also show bike routes, bike shops and landmarks – everything you need to navigate safely and pinpoint specific locations across a large section of the centre of town. If you fancy a set itinerary, turn to A Day On The Bike, also on the front flaps. It takes you on a relaxed 30km (18-mile) route through some of the parts of Copenhagen we haven't featured in the neighbourhood sections, and visits some of the more touristy sights. Pick and choose the bits you fancy, go from back to front, and use the route as it suits you.

A section on Racing and Training (p. 36) fills you in on some of Copenhagen's cycling heritage and provides ideas for longer rides if you want to explore the beautiful countryside around the city, while Essential Bike Info (p. 40) discusses road etiquette and the ins and outs of navigating your way along Copenhagen's cycle routes. Finally, Links and Addresses (p. 44) will give you the practical details you need to know.

COPENHAGEN:
THE CYCLING CITY

Is Copenhagen the most cycling-friendly city in the world? The bike lanes flanking the city's wide boulevards, carrying cyclists away from road traffic and safely to their destinations, would be the envy of most other cities, but Copenhagen is also working hard to make the cyclist's life even better – widening bike lanes, for example, and installing special footplates so cyclists can wait at lights without putting their feet down. The city's town planners and bicycle advocates aim to make Copenhagen the world's best cycling city by 2015 – if it's not already there – and their expertise is sought worldwide by those trying to 'Copenhagenize' their own towns.

The achievements are impressive: 35 per cent of Copenhageners cycle to work (55 per cent in the city centre), jointly pedalling more than 1.2 million km (745,645 miles) a day. All roads feel safe to cycle on, and there are more than 340km (211 miles) of bike lanes throughout the city – both a network of segregated one-way cycle lanes alongside the busy car-carrying corridors, and a developing network of 'green' bicycle routes that take cyclists through parks and green areas, unbothered by cars. If you are on a cycle track on a major route into town, then you may well hit a 'green wave', where the traffic lights during the rush hour are timed to ensure that a cyclist travelling at 20km/h (12 mph) will be swept along on green signals for the length of their trip.

But it wasn't always this way. Although Copenhageners have long been attached to their bikes, after the Second World War rising prosperity and car ownership saw the balance tip in favour of motor vehicles. By the 1960s, the picturesque waterfront at Nyhavn and the main shopping street Strøget (both now pedestrianized) were clogged with cars. Then, in the 1970s, Denmark was hit particularly hard by the fuel crisis. The city instituted car-free Sundays to save petrol, which helped remind residents how pleasant car-free transportation was, adding to the growing environmental movement and existing demands for better cycling infrastructure. The authorities listened, and, despite some opposition, began turning the tide back to bikes.

Nice bike lanes do help, but cycling in Copenhagen (or any other city, for that matter) isn't really about infrastructure. It's about sights, sounds, people, fun: the Copenhagen Cycle Chic blog (copenhagen-cyclechic.com), filled with pictures of fashionable Danes, has made the city's cyclists cool the world over. And Copenhagen itself has so much to offer the cyclist. It's relatively small, but outside the dense old town it's fairly spread out, making the bike the perfect transport for travelling between sights, or from the suburbs into the city. As you pedal you'll see some amazing architecture, from medieval half-timbered buildings to copper-towered Renaissance castles, Gothic, Romantic, Dutch and French influences, as well as the modern functionalism of Arne Jacobsen (whose SAS Hotel sadly has only one suite remaining in an original, Jacobsen-furnished state). Aside from the architecture, there's a real diversity to the city: in an hour's easy pedalling you can visit the grandeur of the historic buildings on Slotsholmen; the furniture warehouses in the docklands area of Refshaleøen, stacked with mid-century-modern design gems; the hippie trails of Christianshavn; and the working abattoirs and louche bars of the meatpacking district.

There is water everywhere, and you'll often find yourself cycling alongside or across it. The city sprawls over several islands and is full of canals, with the three famous lakes to the west separating the centre from the suburbs of Nørrebro and Frederiksberg (technically a town in its own right, though completely encircled by Copenhagen). To the east, the cold, clear Øresund – the strait that forms the border between Denmark and southern Sweden – is never far away. Frequently, too, water falls from the sky, and you may well discover the joys of cycling in the rain – there's no reason not to don a rain cape and cycle on. There are plenty of coffee shops and *smørrebrød* places serving traditional Danish open sandwiches, and world-class museums and galleries where you can take a break. It's what the Danes would do – they're a tremendously practical bunch of cyclists, just getting on with it and riding through everything the Scandinavian weather throws at them. Join them, and Copenhagenize your life…

NEIGHBOURHOODS

CITY

ARCHITECTURE, CULTURE, SHOPPING

Copenhagen's city centre is a dense tangle of old streets, waterways and modern roads, nearly all of which are gloriously navigable by bicycle on safe, traffic-free paths. Bounded by the lakes to the west, it takes in the district of Indre By and Slotsholmen island, the city's historic heart and location of some of its most beautiful buildings. **Christiansborg Palace** ① houses the Danish parliament, while the beautifully warm yellow **Thorvaldsens Museum** ② is dedicated to the nineteenth-century sculptor Bertel Thorvaldsen. The nearby **Ny Carlsberg Glyptotek** ③, founded by the Carlsberg beer dynasty, is home to Copenhagen's best collection of ancient art, as well as works by the Impressionists and sculpture by Rodin and Degas. Also on Slotsholmen is the hidden gem that is the **Royal Library Garden** ④, known as the 'kissing garden'. And shimmering in the water's reflection, the stunning new extension to the **Royal Library** ⑤, or 'Black Diamond', is just one of the ambitious architectural projects lining the harbour.

Not far away on bustling <u>Amagertorv</u>, at one end of <u>Strøget</u>, the main shopping street, you'll find another institution: the flagship store of **Royal Copenhagen** ⑥, the place to go for Denmark's traditional blue-and-white crockery. Amagertorv was once a regular haunt of local miserablist Søren Kierkegaard (he reportedly called it 'the hub of the universe'), and **Café Europa 1989** ⑦ might be a good place for both refreshment and philosophical musings. But the focus here is on design. Other high-end shops include **Illums Bolighus** ⑧ and **Georg Jensen** ⑨, both great for Danish homeware and furniture, while **Hay House** ⑩ showcases mid-century-inspired furniture. Denmark is also renowned for its lighting and lamps, and **Louis Poulsen** ⑪ is one of the best-known brands.

For those wishing to explore Danish design further, the **Dansk Design Center** ⑫ hosts exhibitions devoted to the cutting edge, while the **Designmuseum Danmark** ⑬ provides a comprehensive look at the history of design, particularly furniture. It's on <u>Bredgade</u>, where many of the city's private galleries are located, on the other side of the famous public square, **Kongens Nytorv** ⑭. Try the **Martin Asbæk Gallery** ⑮, which has been representing renowned Danish artists for thirty years. There's also **Cykelmageren** ⑯, a bike boutique

that's almost a gallery in itself. The owner once rode one of his hand-made bikes to London and presented it to the cycle-mad fashion designer Paul Smith.

Other bike-related sights in the area include **Velorbis** ⑰, an upmarket concept shop belonging to the manufacturer of the classic town bikes. **Larry vs Harry** ⑱, close by, where the ultra-fast Bullitt cargo bike was created, is also a cool hangout. Both are near the vibrant Pisserenden neighbourhood. More politely called the Latin Quarter, its network of streets around <u>Studiestrade</u> have long accom-modated a raucous nightlife, and are now home to streetwear brands, vintage and independent shops, and laid-back cafés. **Den Franske Bogcafé** ⑲ sells coffee, as well as French books and films; closer to the university is the excellent **Paludan Bog & Café** ⑳, a huge book-shop with both new and second-hand books. It's a great place to curl up on a rainy day, and has a good café with Wi-Fi. Down the road is **Conditori La Glace** ㉑, Copenhagen's oldest pastry shop and well worth a stop. To end the day, try **Kalaset** ㉒, with its shabby-chic design, good beer and bar food. And, should you want to continue the evening, the minimalist, sophisticated intimacy of cocktail bar **1105** ㉓ might be just the place.

REFUELLING

FOOD
Café Sorgenfri ㉔ is supposedly the oldest *smørrebrød* place in town
Café Sommersko ㉕ for beer, burgers and more

DRINK
Café Hovedtelegrafen ㉖, atop the Post & Tele Museum, has great city views
Café Retro ㉗: cosy, granny-inspired style, staffed by volunteers

WI-FI
The relaxed **Living Room** ㉘ in Pisserenden does brilliant snacks and coffee, and has very comfy sofas

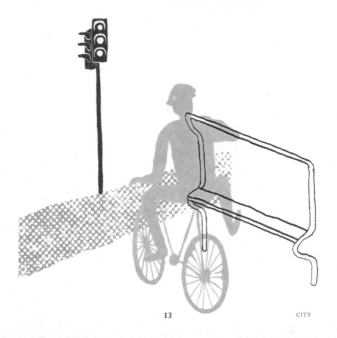

4 mins

½ km   ½ mile   1 km

CADE

MARSTAL

NORDRE FRIHAVNSGADE

LINDE...GADE

NÆSTVEDGADE

PRÆSTØGADE

HOLSTEINSGADE

ØSTBANEGADE

DAMPFÆRGEVEJ

DAMPFÆRGEVEJ

AMERIKAKAJ

AMERIKA PLADS

PAKHUSKAJ

ØSTMOLEN

LANGELINIEKAJ

LANGELINIE ALLÉ

PAKHUSVEJ

MIDTERMOLEN

PAKHUSKAJ

STEEN BILLES GADE

CLASSENSGADE

TYVÆGERGADE

NORDBORGGADE

ARENDALSGADE

KRISTINAGADE

AGGERSBORGGADE

SAABYESVEJ

LIPKESGADE

SØNDERBORGGADE

STAVANGERGADE

INDIAVEJ

INDIAKAJ

LANGELINIEKAJ

FORBINDELSESVEJ

VED NORGESPORTEN

5 👁

DAG HAMMARSKJOLDS ALLÉ

BERGENSGADE

ØSTBANEGADE

TOLDE BUGMANDOVES ALLÉ

OSLO PLADS

6 👁

ØSTELLE

LANGELINIE

NORDRE TOLDBOD

LMAR BRANTINGS PLADS

ESTELLE

VED KONGEPORTEN

KROKODILLEGADE

DRONNINGENS

DELFINGADE

CHURCHILLPARKEN

GRØNNINGEN

ØSTER VOLDGADE

STOKHUSGADE

GERNERSGADE

HAMMERENS GADE

TIGERGADE

ESPLANADEN

AMALIEGADE

1 🚋

RIGENSGADE

GAMMELVAGT

SANKT PAULS PLADS

OLFERT FISCHERS GADE

13 🚋

KLERKEGADE

HINDEGADE

SØLVGADE

FREDERICIAGADE

17

FREDERIKSGADE

NØRREBRO

VINTAGE SHOPS AND BARS

Nørrebro is Copenhagen's answer to Hoxton, Belleville, Prenzlauer Berg, Williamsburg . . . (insert hip neighbourhood here). This is the place to come for vintage clothes and antiques, coffee and bars. The neighbourhood we're describing is broadly bounded by Aboulevard to the south and Tagensvej to the north. Its main street, Nørrebrogade, is lined with restaurants, bars, shops and interesting side streets, and is the busiest bicycling street in the world: 36,000 Copenhageners a day pedal down it, taking advantage of the 'green wave' of traffic lights that lets cyclists flow through without stopping. And the Nørrebro bicycle superhighway is a pleasant, green cycle path that cuts north to south, from **Nørrebroparken** ① to the **Garden of the Royal Danish Veterinarian and Agricultural High School** ②.

Dronning Louises Bro connects the city centre to Nørrebrogade. Cross the bridge and head immediately right onto Ravnsborggade; just across the lake, it's probably the best place to shop for antiques in the city, and is home to more than thirty independent traders who sell everything from bric-à-brac to upmarket retro design (**Ingerslev Antik** ③ is one of the oldest dealers). On Sundays there's also a flea market, and if you get thirsty, there are plenty of bars and cafés – we recommend the authentically jazzy **Kind of Blue** ④. Nearby, **Roxy Klassik** ⑤ is a treasure trove of mid-century-modern Danish furniture and accessories by renowned designers. Follow the road north and you'll find **Nørrebro Bryghus** ⑥, a brew pub that serves good bar food, and **Underwood Ink** ⑦, a bookstore, café and exhibition space with a nice selection of European fiction, much of it in English, and international magazines to read while sipping a coffee.

If continuing shopping, head to Elmegade and Birkegade for cutting-edge womenswear, menswear and jeans brands – try **Goggle** ⑧, **Remö** ⑨ or **Radical Zoo** ⑩. Afterwards take some time out at **Laundromat** ⑪, a café that is also a functioning launderette – perfect for any vintage clothes purchases that need a wash. Just round the corner is **Sankt Hans Torv** ⑫, a popular meeting place. Lock your bike up here, and you're within a stone's throw of scores of cafés, bars and restaurants. South and east of Nørrebrogade, but still close to town, is Blågårdsgade, whose shops and cafés border a leafy park. Blågårds Plads, where **Props** ⑬ makes a good café stop, is architecturally interesting – at one end, the imposing Blågårds Kirke; near the other, the underground **Korsgadehallen** (sports halls) ⑭, designed by BBP Architects and located beneath a landscaped grass hill, down whose slopes the local kids race their sleds in winter.

For good food, try **Radio** ⑮ on the fringes of Frederiksberg. Run by Claus Meyer, co-founder of Noma, it sources all its organic produce and meat locally. Noma chefs, meanwhile, like to eat at **Relæ** ⑯ on Jaegersborggade – both places are leading examples of the 'Nordic Cuisine' movement. Also on Jaegersborggade is **Grød** ⑰, a porridge-only café (nicer than it sounds – *grød* is a Danish speciality, savoury and sweet!). The street is one of Nørrebro's destinations, with bars, restaurants and vintage shops galore – for the latter, we recommend **Resecond** ⑱, while **Mademoistella** ⑲ has vintage clothes and impromptu concerts, and **CMYK kld** ⑳ is a graphic-design gallery. Get to Jaegersborg by cycling through **Assistens Cemetery** ㉑, where Hans Christian Andersen and Søren Kierkegaard are buried, and where Copenhageners chill out on sunny days. To get back into town, head down Stefansgade, where more relaxed bars await.

REFUELLING

FOOD	DRINK
Meyers Bageri ㉒ for great pastries	**Coffee Collective** ㉔: distinctive, stylish roasts
Bodega ㉓ does everything from brunch to beers to DJs at night	**Lyst** ㉕ is a good place to watch the world go by with a beer

WI-FI
Mokkariet ㉖ has vintage furniture, plus a fast Internet connection

VESTERBRO
NIGHTS ON THE TILES AND SLEAZY CHIC

If it's a sex show, a stuffed falcon, vintage designer clothes or some really good coffee you're after, then Vesterbro, the hip western district of Copenhagen, is the place for you. All this and more can be found on its main drag, Istedgade. Still with a dissolute air, the area is now fertile ground for bars, design shops and eclectic boutiques. The Vesterbro we're talking about starts south of the lakes, bounded by Vesterbrogade to the north, and the railway tracks and river to the south. Close to the Bryggebroen bike bridge (leading to Islands Brygge) is **Baisikeli** ①, one of our recommended bike-hire shops, and also a social enterprise. It has another branch in the city centre, but this one has a café.

On your way into Vesterbro from the centre of town, stop in at **Estate Coffee** ② for a shot of their special roasts from small producers, or head up to **Recykel** ③, a beautiful second-hand bike shop, and **Thiemers Magasin** ④, a calm international bookshop that serves good tea. Otherwise, head south to Kødbyen, the meatpacking district, passing by **Mikkeller** ⑤, a fun brew-pub, and **Cofoco** ⑥, also known as Copenhagen Food Consulting, a popular Nordic restaurant. Hidden behind the bright lights of **BioMio** ⑦, a noisily inventive organic restaurant in a former auto-parts showroom, Kødbyen's low-rise complex of white buildings still trades in fresh meat, but also hosts fashionable galleries and bars. **V1** ⑧ has graphic and street art;

Bo Bjerggaard ⑨ was the first of Copenhagen's contemporary galleries to move into the former refrigeration units. Flaesketorvet is also where it happens after dark, with **Jolene** ⑩ providing hipster thrills, and **Karriere** ⑪, with its Olafur Eliasson-designed lights, more upmarket, cocktail-orientated surprises (tip: the bar is actually moving). **Kødbyens Fiskebar** ⑫, close by, is an outstanding seafood restaurant. Back on Istedgade, it's worth a quick pedal up and down the street just to take in the street life and range of shops. **Cykelfabrikken** ⑬ is an upmarket bike boutique, and **Siciliansk Is** ⑭ is perhaps the best ice-cream place in town. Almost opposite, on Skydebanegade, **Sort Kaffe & Vinyl** ⑮ is a coffee shop and record store in one – a firm local favourite. On the other side of Istedgade are clustered **Ichinen** ⑯, for sculptural wooden lighting by Danish designer Tom Rossau, and **Malbeck** ⑰, a wine bar with cool, stepped seating.

Further out of town on Istedgade is **Bang & Jensen** ⑱, the relaxed bar that's credited with kickstarting the area's revival. Just up a side street is **Maur** ⑲, with a carefully curated selection of furniture, homeware and knick-knacks, and **Bob Noon** ⑳, a creative studio that doubles as a shop for arts, crafts and illustration. Run along the same lines, on <u>Vesterbrogade</u>, is **Designer Zoo** ㉑, where eight designers of furniture, jewelry, knitwear and glass work and sell their wares, all in the same space. While pedestrians might not make it down to the quiet far end of Istedgade, take advantage of being on your bike to cycle past the tranquil **Enghavenparken** ㉒ and to the old **Carlsberg Brewery** ㉓. The building is impressive, as are the elephants bestriding the road on <u>Ny Carlsberg Vej</u>. There are art installations in the grounds, and the nearby **Fotografisk Center** ㉔ showcases a range of contemporary and classic photography.

REFUELLING

FOOD
Mother ㉕ does a mean pizza, topped with meat from Kødbyen

Fontana di Trevi ㉖, a small deli with heavenly Italian sandwiches

DRINK
Kaffe ㉗ is a cosy neighbourhood café with good coffee

Dyrehavn ㉘, an atmospheric café/bar with good food and DJs in the evening

WI-FI
Lola's Café ㉙ is on the pleasant Sønder Boulevard

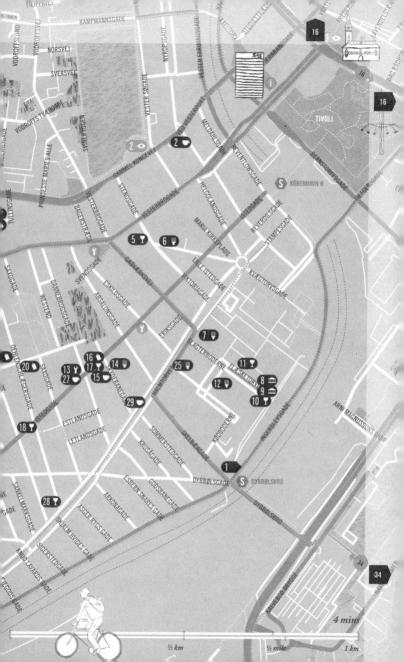

CHRISTIANSHAVN & ISLANDS BRYGGE

LAID-BACK LIFE AND DOCKLANDS

Our Christianshavn and Islands Brygge neighbourhood takes in the islands east of the city centre: Christianshavn itself; Islands Brygge, the harbourfront of Amager island; and the industrial docklands north on Refshaleøen. The area is most easily approached from the distinctive <u>Knippelsbro</u> bridge. Look right as you cross over it, and you might be able to spot the wooden seating of the **Copenhagen Harbour Bath** ①, a landmark swimming spot, jutting into the harbour. Add the nearby **Il Pane di Mauro** ②, a gelateria, and you have one of the city's best summer spots. Make sure you visit the tiny **Retrograd** ③, just off the water, for rare home- and kitch-enware design classics, but for now, keep freewheeling down into Christianshavn proper.

It's easy to see why this former workers' quarter, with its col-ourful cottages and charming cobbled streets, has become one of

Copenhagen's most sought-after addresses. **Lagkagehuset** ④ is a classic Danish bakery, a great place to answer the conundrum, 'what do the Danes call Danishes?' (Answer: *snegls*, or 'snails'.) Keep on going and you'll hit the **Christianshavn canal** ⑤, where you can sit in the sun with your legs over the side and eat that snail. Check out the **Overgaden Institute of Contemporary Art** ⑥ for up-and-coming Danish artists or, if you're feeling energetic, climb the golden spiral staircase of the **Church of Our Saviour** ⑦. It's not for the faint-hearted – the steps are on the outside – but you'll get a great view of the city and the Øresund bridge to Sweden.

Explore the cobbled streets north of the main road and you'll find the **Danish Architecture Centre** ⑧, with interesting small exhibitions. Further north is **Noma** ⑨, where chef René Redzepi's use of unusual, locally sourced ingredients has propelled the restaurant to global celebrity – don't count on turning up without a reservation. Housed in an old mill, on Christianshavn's southern bastion, **Bastionen + Løven** ⑩ is a less exclusive choice for brunch. Also on the water is **Frederiks Bastion** ⑪, a former munitions store that now houses a Nordic-focused art collection and an atmospheric café. Perhaps the area's most famous destination is **Freetown Christiania** ⑫, a former army barracks that is now a semi-autonomous zone within the city. Tumbledown and covered in graffiti, it's alternative but welcoming (except on the self-explanatory <u>Pusher Street</u>, where you should not take any photos). Behind Christiania, the waterfront paths make pretty riding – check A Day On The Bike on the front flaps for a route through the hippy housing on the opposite shore.

Bike tourists should visit **Christiania Smedie** ⑬, the birthplace of the Christiania bike, those load-carrying trikes used to transport everything from groceries to children. You'll spot them all around Copenhagen, and in boho urban neighbourhoods worldwide. Nearby, **Christiania Cycles** ⑭ is home to the famous Pedersen bicycles, with their pyramid-esque design and hammock seat. Outside Christiania, but not far away, is the **Bicycle Innovation Lab** ⑮, Denmark's first cultural centre for bicycles, which hosts regular exhibitions and has a 'bicycle library' where you can test-drive new designs. Before leaving, be sure to head north up to Refshaleøen island, where the former Burmeister & Wain shipyards are now home to galleries such as **Yard** ⑯ and **Københavns Yacht Service** ⑰. Poke your nose in, and you'll

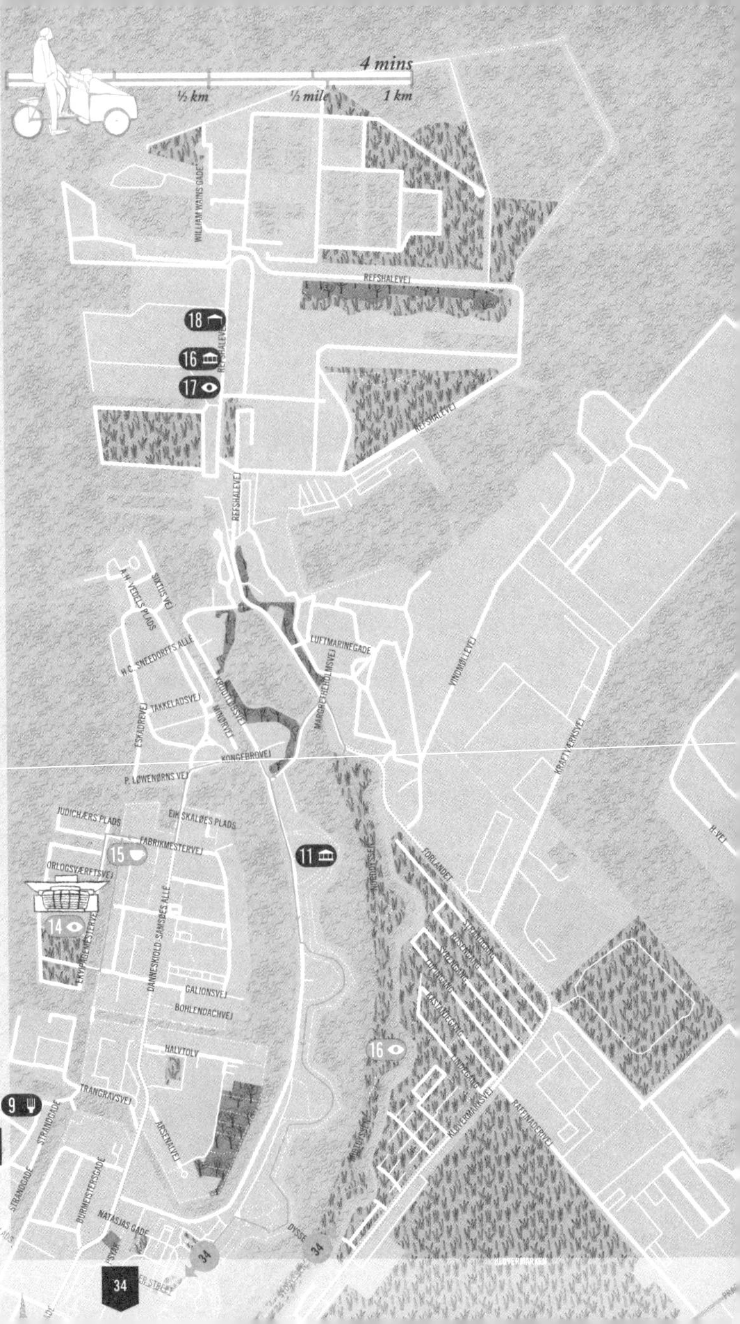

4 mins

½ km   ½ mile   1 km

WILLIAM WAINS GADE

REFSHALEVEJ

18 🏛

16 🏛

17 👁

REFSHALEVEJ

REFSHALEVEJ

PROVIANTVEJ

BÅTTEVEJ

A.H. VEDELS PLADS

W.C. SNEEDORFFS ALLÉ

FISK TORPVEJ

TAKKELADSVEJ

MINØRVEJ

KONGEBROVEJ

LUFTMARINEGADE

KRØYERS VEJ

H. VEJ

P. LØWENØRNS VEJ

JUDICHÆRS PLADS

EIK SKALØES PLADS

FABRIKMESTERVEJ

FORLANDET

15 🏛

ORLOGSVÆRFTSVEJ

DANNESKIOLD SAMSØES ALLÉ

11 🏛

14 👁

GALIONSVEJ

BOHLENDACHVEJ

HALVTOLV

16 👁

TRANGRAVSVEJ

ARSENALVEJ

9 🍴

16

STRANDGADE

BURMEISTERSGADE

BURMEISTERSGADE

NATASJAS GADE

DYSSE

34

34

see boats from floor to ceiling. The main attraction, however, is the **Refshaleøen flea market** ⑱, on even Sundays of the month, in a gargantuan warehouse full of mid-century Danish teak furniture, lamps, accessories and homeware.

Finally, if you're feeling adventurous, head off map to **Amager Strandpark** ⑲, the beach where Copenhageners go to run, rollerblade, windsurf and picnic whenever the sun's out – just follow <u>Øresundsvej</u> east. Or head south down <u>Ørestads Boulevard</u>, where after a couple of kilometres you'll find **8Tallet** ⑳, a housing project containing 475 homes, designed by the Bjarne Ingels Group and shaped like a figure of eight. It's landscaped for maximum light, with sloped gardens up all eleven storeys and a wide walkway extending from top to bottom. There are panoramic views, and a café at the far end to refuel for the ride back.

REFUELLING

FOOD	DRINK
Luna's Diner ㉑ for a healthy brunch or a good burger	Eiffel Bar, a locals' bar in the heart of Christianshavn ㉒

WI-FI
Sweet Treat for coffee, cake or a light meal with Wi-Fi ㉓

RACING AND TRAINING

Denmark may not have the cycle-sport heritage of some of its European neighbours to the south, but its capital city has been one of the formative sites of the World Cycling Championships, hosting it a total of five times – more than any other location. In 2011, it was the site of Mark Cavendish's memorable victory in the men's road race and Giorgia Bronzini's second consecutive win in the women's event. The time trials (won by Germany's Tony Martin and Judith Arndt) started and finished in front of the town hall, while the men's road race set off from the city centre and headed north to a circuit in Rundersdal, the 'vegetable garden of Copenhagen', where the women and juniors also competed. Before that, the World Championships hadn't visited since 1956, when Rik Van Steenbergen spearheaded a Belgian assault that bagged three of the top four places. The three earlier races were held in 1949, when Steenbergen also won, beating Ferdi Kübler and Fausto Coppi; in 1937, a race in which only eight cyclists finished; and in 1931, the year that the UCI responded to the Italians' previous dominance (through the use of what were then considered unsportsmanlike team tactics) by staging the race as an individual time trial. Despite this, it was an Italian – Learco 'the Locomotive' Guerro – who triumphed.

None of the Grand Tours has visited Copenhagen, the closest being the Giro d'Italia's visit to Herning, in western Denmark, in 2012. The Danmark Rundt, however, usually finishes in town – or Frederiksberg, to be precise. Among those to have won it since it began in 1985 are David Millar, Tyler Hamilton and Denmark's own Bjarne Riis; other Danish victors include Jesper Skibby and Jakob Fuglsang, who holds the record with three wins. Denmark has strong representation in the ranks of the professional *peloton*. Rolf Sørensen is the most successful Danish cyclist of all, winning two Tour de France stages, as well as the Tour of Flanders and the Liège–Bastogne–Liège, during the 1990s. Bjarne Riis's overall victory in the 1996 Tour de France (which despite his later admission of doping is still recognized by the UCI) is Denmark's only Grand Tour win; Riis now manages the Saxo-Tinkoff team, which is based in Lyngby just outside Copenhagen. Brian Holm, once a loyal *domestique* for Riis, among others, when not on the road as a *directeur sportif* for the Belgian Omega Pharma-QuickStep team, still lives in his native Copenhagen.

On an amateur level, the club scene in Denmark is strong. **Frederiksberg Bane- og Landevejsklub**, **Amager Cykle Ring** and **Ordrup Cykle Club** are popular clubs in the Copenhagen region, but to join their club rides you really need to be a member. However, one of our recommended road-bike shops, **Soigneur**, holds Wednesday evening training rides between April and August. Soigneur is on Strandvejen: cycle up Østerbrogade and the road will turn into Strandvejen; after 500m (1,640 ft) you'll cross a railway bridge and the shop is on the right. The rides are open to riders of all levels: groups are split into 'caffe-latte' pace, mid-pace and 'puking', for those who want to go really fast. The traditional post-ride coffee stop is at the scenic **Café Jorden Rundt**, further up Strandvejen, but another good coffee stop is **Ourselves Alone**, in the city centre. Soigneur is a good bet for any spares and repairs you might need, as are **Bikebuster** and **Ben Ben,** both on Vesterbrogade. Full details can be found in the Links and Addresses section, along with links to recommended racing and training routes.

If you prefer to do your cycling in organized events, the recently revived **Aarhus–Copenhagen** ride might be for you. In 2012, over 4,500 riders competed over the full 375km (233-mile) route or a 190km (118-mile) version, starting in Odense and crossing the 6.7km (4 mile)-long Great Belt Bridge between the islands of Funen and Zealand – the first time bicycles had been allowed onto the bridge. The **Ritter Classic,** named after Ole Ritter, is a closed-road sportive that takes place in June. Copenhagen also has a world-class velodrome at the **Ballerup Super Arena**, which functions as a training base for the national team and is home to the **Copenhagen Six Day** in February. At the other end of the scale, the tradition of *Svajerløb* (cargo-bike races) was revived by the creators of the Bullitt cargo bike, **Larry vs Harry** (p. 12), and the **Firmacyklen** bike shop. Last raced in 1960, *Svajerløb* used to be hotly contested by the city's delivery boys and messengers. Traditionally, competitors in the two- and three-wheeler categories raced one 'empty' lap, and then stopped to load car tyres, newspaper bundles and a secret cargo before riding two more laps while fully loaded.

ESSENTIAL BIKE INFO

Denmark is second only to the Netherlands on the list of safest cycling countries. Everyone cycles in Copenhagen. Goods are delivered, shopping carried and kids transported to school, tucked under blankets on Christiania bikes and Dutch *bakfiets*. The biggest obstacle you may notice is the sheer number of bicycles on the streets!

ETIQUETTE

The Danes are, by and large, very careful cyclists, respectful of traffic laws and courteous to others. Here are some tips to help you fit in:

- Copenhagen's cyclists are very hot on hand signals, so don't forget to indicate that you're turning. Also, raise your hand next to your face, palm facing forward, if you're going to stop.
- It is illegal for cyclists to filter across the traffic lanes when turning left at a crossroads (across the opposite lane of traffic). Instead, you must perform a 'box turn'. To do this, stay on the right side of your lane, cross the junction to the far side, signal that you are stopping and tuck in to the right, in front of the cyclists waiting at the red light. Then, when the lights change, simply ride away (see diagram opposite).
- Stay to the right of any bike lane you are riding in to allow other cyclists to pass – if you hear a bell behind you, it's probably because you're in the way. And if you're overtaking someone yourself, check over your left shoulder to make sure there's nobody speeding up behind you.
- Don't go the wrong way down bike lanes. There will almost certainly be a lane on the other side of the road for travel in the correct direction.
- Stop and wait when the traffic lights (including the special bicycle traffic lights) are against you – though turning right when the lights are red is tolerated.

SAFETY

Copenhagen is very safe on a bike, and cars will unfailingly be aware of your presence. Drivers turning across a segregated bike path will not encroach on your space; this is as true of cars travelling in the same direction as you as of those crossing a bike lane at a junction. But there are a few things to watch out for:

- Use lights after dark – the police disapprove of people who don't.
- Bikes are often allowed up one-way streets in contraflow to the car traffic. Look out for the road markings, a sign showing a bike and the word *undtaget* (which means 'excepted', indicating it's OK to cycle the wrong way up the street). Check our maps if you're in any doubt.
- Do not walk in bike lanes – they are reserved for faster-moving traffic and you risk getting bumped into.

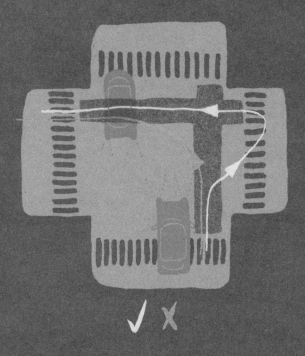

SECURITY

Although locals would say that Copenhagen suffers from high levels of bike theft, it seems safer than many other cities. The introduction of wheel locks to all town bicycles sold in Denmark after 1993 caused a large fall in thefts, and now it is primarily unlocked or very expensive bikes that get stolen. A particular target is valuable cargo bikes, though this shouldn't be of concern to out-of-towners.

Always lock your bike, even if you are just popping into a shop. If you've hired a bike, use the lock provided, and if you've brought your own expensive bicycle, make sure it's securely locked to something immovable.

FINDING YOUR WAY

Copenhagen doesn't actually have much signage for cyclists, and for a small city, it is quite spread out. It is very low rise, and there aren't that many landmarks around, but outside the dense and twisting old town, the roads tend to be straight and easy to navigate. It's unlikely you'll find yourself in a part of town where you can't stop and ask for advice, and often there are street maps and information points in the suburbs. Because it is low rise, the various churches and the Radisson SAS Hotel make good navigation aids.

CITY BIKES AND BIKE HIRE

Copenhagen was the first city to introduce municipal city bikes – strange, unwieldy solid-wheeled things, available from May until September, released from their stands by the insertion of a refundable 20-kroner piece (about £2). They were free to use in central Copenhagen, with no time restrictions. In 2013, however, they are no longer on the streets due to a lack of funding – the city council says money will be spent instead on bike lanes and infrastructure – and their long-term future is in doubt.

For bike hire, we recommend **Baisikeli** (p. 24). The company repairs and renovates old bikes, hiring some out and sending many more to Mozambique to provide low-cost mobility (employees also spend time every year in Africa, teaching locals valuable skills). It has two locations in Copenhagen: one in the city centre and one in Vesterbro, which is the main workshop. Alternatively, try **Københavns Cykelbørs** in the centre of town.

OTHER PUBLIC TRANSPORT

It is possible to take bikes on the **Copenhagen Metro**, as long as you buy a bicycle ticket. And since 2010, in a move to promote mixed-mode commuting, bikes travel free on Copenhagen's S trains, the urban transit system that stretches further into the suburbs. A maximum of two bicycles are allowed on any of the city's S and R buses, but some of the harbour bus lines (boats) do not accept bikes. Do not expect to take bikes on public transport in rush hours – between 7 and 9am, or 3:30 and 5:30pm.

All taxis are required by law to carry a bike rack, so if you've had one too many, or it's raining cats and dogs, consider taking a taxi instead. Like everything else in Copenhagen, taxis are expensive, but the additional fee to take a bike is small.

TRAVELLING TO COPENHAGEN WITH BIKES

Copenhagen is well served by international trains through Germany, which connect to the international rail network at Cologne and Hamburg. Be aware that German high-speed ICE trains do not allow bike bags bigger than 85cm (33 in.) in any dimension, which practically rules out any non-folding bikes. The slower German Intercity and Eurocity (IC and EC) trains, however, do allow bikes to be wheeled on board if you pay for a reservation, or carried in a regular-sized bag. There's also a night sleeper to Copenhagen, which follows these more relaxed rules. All trains allow folding bikes, though on ICE trains these must be bagged.

Copenhagen Airport is located in Amager, and it is entirely possible to cycle from the airport into the centre of town. It's only 8km (5 miles) from the city centre, and can be found at the southern end of Kastrupvej (follow it off the edge of our map; see p. 35).

LINKS AND ADDRESSES

1105
Kristen Bernikows Gade 4, 1105
1105.dk

8Tallet
Richard Mortensens Vej 81, 2300
8tallet.dk

Amager Strandpark
Jollevej, 2300
amager-strand.dk

Assistens Cemetery
Kapelvej 4, 2200
assistens.dk

Bang & Jensen
Istedgade 130, 1650
blog.bangogjensen.dk

Bastionen + Loven
Christianshavns Voldgade 50,
1424
bastionen-loven.dk

BioMio
Halmtorvet 19, 1700
biomio.dk

Bo Bjerggaard
Flæsketorvet 85 A, 1711
bjerggaard.com

Bob Noon
Matthæusgade 21, 1666
bobnoon.dk

Bodega
Kapelvej 1, 2200
bodega.dk

Botanical Garden
Gothersgade 128, 1353
botanik.snm.ku.dk

Café Europa 1989
Amagertorv 1, 1160
europa1989.dk

Café Hovedtelegrafen
Købmagergade 37, 1150
cafehovedtelegrafen.dk

Café Jorden Rundt
Strandvejen 152,
2920 Charlottenlund
cafejordenrundt.dk

Café Retro
Knabrostræde 26, 1210
cafe-retro.dk

Café Skildpadden
Gråbrødretorv 9, 1154
skildpadden.dk

Café Sommersko
Kronprinsensgade 6, 1114
sommersko.dk

Café Sorgenfri
Brolæggerstræde 8, 1211
cafesorgenfri.dk

Carlsberg Brewery
Ny Carlsberg Vej 100, 1799
visitcarlsberg.dk

Christiansborg Palace
Prins Jørgens Gård 1, 1218
christiansborg.dk

Church of Our Saviour
Sankt Annæ Gade 29, 1416
visitcopenhagen.com

CMYK kld
Jægersborggade 51, 2200
butikcmyk.dk

Coffee Collective
Jægersborggade 10, 2200
coffeecollective.dk

Cofoco
Abel Cathrines Gade 7, 1654
cofoco.dk

Conditori La Glace
Skoubogade 3, 1158
laglace.dk

Copenhagen City Hall
Rådhuspladsen 1, 1566
kk.dk

Copenhagen Harbour Bath
Islands Brygge 7, 2300
visitcopenhagen.com

Copenhagen Opera House
Ekvipagemestervej 10, 1438
kglteater.dk

Danish Architecture Centre
Strandgade 27b, 1401
dac.dk

Dansk Design Center
H. C. Andersens Blvd 27, 1553
ddc.dk

Den Franske Bogcafé
Fiolstræde 16, 1171
denfranskebogcafe.dk

Den Franske Café
Sortedam Dossering 101, 2100
denfranskecafe.dk

Designer Zoo
Vesterbrogade 137, 1620
dzoo.dk

Designmuseum Danmark
Bredgade 68, 1260
designmuseum.dk

Dyrehavn
Sønder Boulevard 72, 1720
dyrehavenkbh.dk

Eiffel Bar
Wildersgade 58, 1408
eiffelbar.dk

Estate Coffee
Gammel Kongevej 1, 1610
estatecoffee.dk

Fontana di Trevi
Vesterbrogade 87, 1620
fontana-di-trevi.dk

Forno a Legna
Falkoner Allé 42, 2300

Fotografisk Center
Pasteursvej 14, 1799
photography.dk

Frederiks Bastion
Refshalevej 80, 1432
frederiksbastion.dk

Frederiksberg Gardens
Frederiksberg, 2000
ses.dk

Freetown Christiania
christiania.org

**Garden of the Royal Danish
Veterinarian and Agricultural
High School**
1870 Frederiksberg
science.ku.dk

Georg Jensen
Amagertorv 4, 1160
georgjensen.com

Goggle
Elmegade 3, 2200
goggle-theshop.com

Granola
Værnedamsvej 5,
1819 Frederiksberg

Grød
Jægersborggade 50, 2200
groed.com

Hay House
Østergade 61, 1100
hay.dk

Ichinen
Istedgade 59, 1650
tomrossau.dk

Il Pane di Mauro
Islands Brygge 23, 2300
ilpanedimauro.dk

Jolene
Flæsketorvet 81, 1711

Illums Bolighus
Amagertorv 10, 1160
illumsbolighus.dk

Ingerslev Antik
Ravnsborggade 6, 2200
ingerslevantik.dk

Kaffe
Istedgade 90, 1650
kaffeistedgade.dk

Kalaset
Vendersgade 16, 1363

Karriere
Flæsketorvet 57, 1711
karrierebar.com

Kartoffelrækkerne
Østerbro, 2100
kartoffelraekkerne.dk

Kind of Blue
Ravnsborggade 17, 2200
kindofblue.dk

Københavns Yacht Service
Refshalevej 163, 1432
yachtgarage.dk

Kødbyens Fiskebar
Flæsketorvet 100, 1711
fiskebaren.dk

Kontiki Bar
Takkelloftvej, 1437
kontikibar.dk

Korsgadehallen
Korsgade 29, 2200
kulturogfritid.kk.dk

Lagkagehuset
Torvegade 45, 1400
lagkagehuset.dk

Laundromat
Elmegade 15, 2200
thelaundromatcafe.com

Little Mermaid
Langelinie, 2100
mermaidsculpture.dk

Living Room
Larsbjørnsstræde 17, 1454
trendliving.dk

Lola's Café
Sønder Boulevard 30, 1720
lolascafe.dk

Louis Poulsen
Gammel Strand 28, 1202
louispoulsen.com

Luna's Diner
Sankt Annæ Gade 5, 1416
lunasdiner.dk

Lyst
Stefansgade 41, 2200

Mademoistella
Jægersborggade 52, 2200
mademoistella.tumblr.com

Malbeck
Istedgade 61, 1650
malbeck.dk

Martin Asbæk Gallery
Bredgade 23, 1260
martinasbaek.com

Maur
Oehlenschlægersgade 32, 1663
maur.dk

Meyers Bageri
Jægersborggade 9, 2200
clausmeyer.dk

Mikkeller
Viktoriagade 8, 1655
mikkeller.dk

Mokkariet
Jagtvej 127, 2200

Mother
Høkerboderne 9, 1712
mother.dk

Noma
Strandgade 93, 1401
noma.dk

Normann
Østerbrogade 70, 2100
normann-copenhagen.com

Nørrebro Bryghus
Ryesgade 3, 2200
noerrebrobryghus.dk

Ny Carlsberg Glyptotek
Dantes Plads 7, 1556
glyptoteket.dk

Ourselves Alone
Badstuestræde 7, 1209
ourselvesalone.dk

Overgaden Institute of Contemporary Art
Overgaden Neden V
andet 17, 1414
overgaden.org

Paludan Bog & Café
Fiolstræde 10, 1171
paludan-cafe.dk

Props
Blågårdsgade 5, 2200
propscoffeeshop.dk

Radical Zoo
Elmegade 19, 2200
radical-zoo.com

Radio
Julius Thomsens Gade 12, 1632
restaurantradio.dk

Refshaleøen flea market
Refshalevej 163, 1432

Remö
Elmegade 3, 2200
remo.dk

Resecond
Jægersborggade 49, 2200
resecond.com

Restaurant Relæ
Jægersborggade 41, 2200
restaurant-relae.dk

Retrograd
Gunløgsgade 7, 2300

Royal Copenhagen
Amagertorv 6, 1160
royalcopenhagen.com

Royal Library
Søren Kierkegaards Plads 1, 1219
kb.dk

Royal Library Garden
Søren Kierkegaards Plads 1, 1221
ses.dk

Roxy Klassik
Fælledvej 4, 2200
roxyklassik.dk

Siciliansk Is
Skydebanegade 3, 1709
sicilianskis.dk

Soigneur
Strandvejen 6, 2100
soigneur.dk

Sort Kaffe & Vinyl
Skydebanegade 4, 1709
sortkaffeogvinyl.dk

Statens Museum for Kunst
Sølvgade 48–50, 1307
smk.dk

Sweet Treat
Sankt Annæ Gade 3a, 1416
sweettreat.dk

Thiemers Magasin
Tullinsgade 24, 1618
thiemersmagasin.dk

Thorvaldsens Museum
Bertel Thorvaldsens Plads
2, 1213
thorvaldsensmuseum.dk

Torvehallerne
Frederiksborggade 21, 1360
torvehallernekbh.dk

Tycho Brahe Planetarium
Gammel Kongevej 10, 1610
planetariet.dk

Underwood Ink
Ryesgade 30a, 2200
underwood-ink.com

V1 Gallery
Flæsketorvet 69, 1711
v1gallery.com

Yard Gallery
Refshalevej 163, 1432
yardgallery.dk

BIKES SHOPS, CLUBS, RACES AND VENUES

For links to our racing and
training routes, please visit
citycyclingguides.com

Aarhus–Copenhagen
aarhus-copenhagen.com

Amager Cykle Ring
Saltværksvej 56, 2770 Kastrup
amagercr.dk

Baisikeli
• Turesensgade 10, 1368
• Ingerslevsgade 80, 1705
baisikeli.dk

Ballerup Super Arena
Ballerup Idrætsby 4,
2750 Ballerup
ballerupsuperarena.dk

Ben Ben
Vesterbrogade 55, 1620
benben.dk

Bicycle Innovation Lab
Holmbladsgade 71, 2300
bicycleinnovationlab.dk

Bikebuster
Vesterbrogade 165, 1800
Frederiksberg
bikebuster.dk

Christiania Cycles
Refshalevej 2, 1432
pedersen-bike.dk

Christiania Smedie
Mælkevejen 83, 1440
christianiabikes.dk

Copenhagen Six Day
6dageslob.dk

Cykelfabrikken
Istedgade 92, 1650
cykelfabrikken.dk

Cykelmageren
Store Kongensgade 57, 1264
cykelmageren.dk

Firmacyklen
Rhodesiavej 74, 2770 Kastrup
firmacyklen.dk

**Frederiksberg Bane-
og Landevejsklub**
Frederiksvej 14,
2000 Frederiksberg
fbl-cykling.dk

Københavns Cykelbørs
Gothersgade 157, 1123
cykelborsen.dk

Larry vs Harry
Frederiksborggade 41, 1361
larryvsharry.com

Ordrup Cykle Club
Jægersborg Allé 148 B,
2900 Gentofte
ordrupcc.dk

Recykel
Tullinsgade 10, 1618
recykel.dk

Ritter Classic
ritterclassic.dk

Velorbis
Nørre Farimagsgade 63, 1364
velorbis.com

OTHER USEFUL SITES

Copenhagen Airport
Lufthavnsboulevarden 6,
2770 Kastrup
cph.dk

Copenhagen Metro
intl.m.dk

NOTES

Rapha, established in London, has always been a champion of city cycling – from testing our first prototype jackets on the backs of bike couriers, to a whole range of products designed specifically for the demands of daily life on the bike. As well as an online emporium of products, films, photography and stories, Rapha has a growing network of Cycle Clubs, locations around the globe where cyclists can enjoy live racing, food, drink and products. Rapha is also the official clothing supplier of Team Sky, the world's leading cycling team.